GUIDE

MW01113782

higher education & campus ministry

Connecting with Students in Schools, Colleges, and Campus Ministries

Division of Higher Education
General Board of Higher Education and Ministry

HIGHER EDUCATION AND CAMPUS MINISTRY

Copyright © 2012 by Cokesbury

This book is printed on acid-free paper.

ISBN 978-1-426-73677-3

Some paragraph numbers for and language in the Book of Discipline *may have changed in the 2012 revision, which was published after these Guidelines were printed. We regret any inconvenience.*

MANUFACTURED IN THE UNITED STATES OF AMERICA

Contents

Called to a Ministry of Faithfulness and Vitality

Y ou are so important to the life of the Christian church! You have consented to join with other people of faith who, through the millennia, have sustained the church by extending God's love to others. You have been called and have committed your unique passions, gifts, and abilities to a position of leadership. This Guideline will help you understand the basic elements of that ministry within your own church and within The United Methodist Church.

Leadership in Vital Ministry

Each person is called to ministry by virtue of his or her baptism, and that ministry takes place in all aspects of daily life, both in and outside of the church. Your leadership role requires that you will be a faithful participant in the **mission of the church,** which is to partner with God to **make disciples of Jesus Christ for the transformation of the world.** You will not only engage in your area of ministry, but will also work to empower others to be in ministry as well. The vitality of your church, and the Church as a whole, depends upon the faith, abilities, and actions of all who work together for the glory of God.

Clearly then, as a pastoral leader or leader among the laity, your ministry is not just a "job," but a spiritual endeavor. You are a spiritual leader now, and others will look to you for spiritual leadership. What does this mean?

All persons who follow Jesus are called to grow spiritually through the practice of various Christian habits (or "means of grace") such as prayer, Bible study, private and corporate worship, acts of service, Christian conferencing, and so on. Jesus taught his disciples practices of spiritual growth and leadership that you will model as you guide others. As members of the congregation grow through the means of grace, they will assume their own role in ministry and help others in the same way. This is the cycle of disciple making.

The Church's Vision

While there is one mission—to make disciples of Jesus Christ—the portrait of a successful mission will differ from one congregation to the next. One of your roles is to listen deeply for the guidance and call of God in your own context. In your church, neighborhood, or greater community, what are the greatest needs? How is God calling your congregation to be in a ministry of service and witness where they are? What does vital ministry look like in the life of your congregation and its neighbors? What are the characteristics, traits, and actions that identify a person as a faithful disciple in your context? This portrait, or vision, is formed when you and the other leaders discern together how your gifts from God come together to fulfill the will of God.

Assessing Your Efforts

We are generally good at deciding what to do, but we sometimes skip the more important first question of what we want to accomplish. Knowing your task (the mission of disciple making) and knowing what results you want (the vision of your church) are the first two steps in a vital ministry. The third step is in knowing how you will assess or measure the results of what you do and who you are (and become) because of what you do. Those measures relate directly to mission and vision, and they are more than just numbers.

One of your leadership tasks will be to take a hard look, with your team, at all the things your ministry area does or plans to do. No doubt they are good and worthy activities; the question is, *"Do these activities and experiences lead people into a mature relationship with God and a life of deeper discipleship?"* That is the business of the church, and the church needs to do what only the church can do. You may need to eliminate or alter some of what you do if it does not measure up to the standard of faithful disciple making. It will be up to your ministry team to establish the specific standards against which you compare all that you do and hope to do. (This Guideline includes further help in establishing goals, strategies, and measures for this area of ministry.)

The Mission of The United Methodist Church

Each local church is unique, yet it is a part of a *connection,* a living organism of the body of Christ. Being a connectional Church means in part that all United Methodist churches are interrelated through the structure and organization of districts, conferences, and jurisdictions in the larger "family" of the denomination. *The Book of Discipline of The United Methodist Church* describes, among other things, the ministry of all United Methodist Christians, the essence of servant ministry and leadership, how to organize and accomplish that ministry, and how our connectional structure works (see especially ¶¶126–138).

Our Church extends way beyond your doorstep; it is a global Church with both local and international presence. You are not alone. The resources of the entire denomination are intended to assist you in ministry. With this help and the partnership of God and one another, the mission continues. You are an integral part of God's church and God's plan!

(For help in addition to this Guideline and the *Book of Discipline*, see "Resources" at the end of your Guideline, www.umc.org, and the other websites listed on the inside back cover.)

Your Part in Higher Education and Campus Ministry

t hank you for taking on leadership in your church for higher education and campus ministry. Elected by the charge conference for a one-year term, you are a member of the council on ministries, or the church council, and the charge conference. You are responsible for interpreting and recommending to the church council ways for implementing the church's mission in higher education and campus ministry. You work with the guidance of the pastor and the chairperson of the church council.

You are also the person on the "front line" in the important work of identifying and developing leadership for the church and for the world. You are the one in the local church who takes a large view on developing the next generation of leaders.

Everything you do—from helping make connections between students and campus ministers to encouraging students to consider attending a United Methodist-related college to supporting the Black College Fund and Africa University—is important and makes a difference in the quality of leadership in the future. It is essential for the future of The United Methodist Church that students are nurtured in their faith during their college years.

College is a time when students shape the dreams and visions that will influence the rest of their lives. Those years also are a time when students examine the faith and values that will support their life choices. Your ministry helps students know that the church supports them as they increase in knowledge and shape those visions. That is no small responsibility!

Your Role

The responsibility is not yours alone; it is shared with a team of individuals working together to advocate for the church's ministry in higher education. You are the team leader for your congregation. Prayerfully gather a group of people to join you in this ministry. In large churches, a committee may have been appointed to work with you. In small churches, you may be the only one officially designated with responsibility for higher education and campus ministry. Invite people to join in the work. Parents, teachers, students, college contacts, and high school guidance counselors could be invaluable members of the team.

At first, your responsibilities may seem overwhelming. This booklet will help you understand the scope of your work. It will also give you practical resources for doing that work.

As chair of the ministry team on higher education and campus ministry, your work is wide-ranging. Recruit others in your church to assist you with these responsibilities:

- advocating within your congregation for the importance of the mission of the church's work in higher education: to identify and develop strong future leaders for the church and the world
- keeping the church council aware of higher education and campus ministry concerns
- promoting local church support for the higher education and campus ministry programs of your annual conference and of the Division of Higher Education of the General Board of Higher Education and Ministry
- interpreting and promoting the Black College Fund and the Hispanic, Asian, and Native American (HANA) educational ministries
- recruiting students for United Methodist-related colleges and encouraging students to participate in United Methodist campus ministry units on other private and public colleges
- planning your church's ministry to and with college and university students, staff, faculty, and administrators
- encouraging local support of United Methodist-related colleges, universities, and campus ministries in your annual conference
- helping to link students with United Methodist-supported campus ministries and with the United Methodist Student Movement
- promoting the United Methodist Student Loans and Scholarships programs through the observance of United Methodist Student Day, World Communion Sunday, and Native American Ministries Sunday offerings
- alerting the pastor, parents, and students to the availability of loans and scholarships for United Methodist students through the Office of Loans and Scholarships of the General Board of Higher Education and Ministry, the United Methodist Higher Education Foundation, your annual conference, and your local church.

Many resources for your work are listed in this guide. They include information about the history of United Methodism, our educational ministries, interpretation of higher education and campus ministry programs, a sample calendar of a year's program ideas, and printed, video, Internet, and personal resources.

One resource that will be especially valuable is *Interpreter* magazine, the church's program journal for local church leaders. Seven copies are sent free to each church; these may be sent to church leaders' home addresses. Additional subscriptions are available. Order from United Methodist Communications, PO Box 310, 810 Twelfth Avenue South, Nashville, TN 37202-0320; website: www.interpretermagazine.org. Also, you may access *Interpreter* magazine articles online at their website.

Resources and information regarding United Methodist higher education ministries can be found on the Internet. The main address is www.gbhem.org. From there, you can go to specific pages about higher education issues, institutions, resources, and campus ministries.

The staff of the Division of Higher Education is available to answer questions and discuss issues. The mailing address is PO Box 340007, Nashville, TN 37203-0007; telephone is 615-340-7402; e-mail at scu@gbhem.org. A directory of information available on the Internet can be found on pages 27–28.

So, How Do You Get Started?

One place to begin understanding your congregation's ministry in higher education is to recognize each local church's responsibility for "planning and implementing a program of nurture, outreach, and witness for persons and families within and without the congregation" (¶ 242, *Book of Discipline*). Within and beyond your congregation, there are individuals who are on the college campus and engaged in higher education. You and your church have the opportunity to develop creative ministries of nurture, outreach, and witness with and for these people.

A strong program in higher education and campus ministry in your church must have the understanding and support of key persons. It is important to consult with your pastor and the chairperson of the church council. In a small church, one person may well be able to manage this ministry area. In middle-sized churches, task forces could help plan and promote special events. In larger churches, a standing commission might be in order. Even then, special events for students who are home from college may call for subcommittees or task forces.

The way you organize your work will affect all that you do. As you read this guide, make notes to help you choose the best approach for accomplishing your tasks. Most importantly, think prayerfully about the best way to minister to persons in higher education. Then put your plans and ideas to work.

Here are some ways to begin:

- **Request resources.** The Division of Higher Education of the General Board of Higher Education and Ministry provides many resources and information at www.gbhem.org. In addition, you can search the data base for information about United Methodist-related higher education institutions and ministries for students on campuses through www.gbhem.org/findyourplace.

- **Identify your constituents.** High school sophomores, juniors, and seniors are potential candidates for United Methodist-related colleges, universities, and campus ministries. Get to know high school counselors who assist students in their college planning. Students now at college at both the undergraduate and the graduate level are also important constituents. Identify any college administrators, faculty, staff members, and trustees who are related to your church. College chaplains and campus ministers are valuable sources of information. Remember, too, that commuter students in your congregation are also candidates.

- **Connect with your annual conference Board of Higher Education and Campus Ministry.** Each annual conference has a board or equivalent structure to provide for the connection relationships between the Division of Higher Education, higher education institutions within the conference and local churches. Find out about existing programs and how your church can be involved in supporting higher education initiatives.

- **Investigate the history of your church's support** for the UM-related school, college, or university in your annual conference and for the apportioned educational funds of the Black College Fund, the Ministerial Education Fund, and Africa University. Share this with your church's leaders. Find ways to increase your church's giving.

- **Talk with others in the congregation about ministry in higher education.** Listen to their concerns for students, staff, and faculty at colleges. What are their ideas for making your local church's ministry in higher education an important and creative part of the lives of those who are studying, teaching, or working at colleges and universities? Perhaps there are people in your local church who would covenant to pray regularly for this ministry, asking God to lead your church to be involved in ministry in higher education in new ways.

To get started immediately, go to "Higher Education, Campus Ministry, and Your Local Church" on pages 21–22. Read through the suggestions, choose one or two that appeal to you, and get started.

Our Church's Call to Be Involved in Higher Education

the United Methodist has a historic and impressive history in higher learning. As early as the mid-1700s, John Wesley and his Methodist friends began founding schools and tutoring children and others who otherwise were denied the opportunity to develop their God-given talent. It is this concern for people that brings United Methodists into ministry in higher education.

The United Methodist Church today continues a 250-year tradition of ministry in education. John Wesley began the Holy Club and the Methodist Society with a student at Kings College, Oxford University. The Methodist movement itself was born on a college campus. Wesley was a tireless reader, writer, translator, and book and pamphlet publisher. He founded Kingswood School, the first Methodist educational institution in England, in 1748.

When The Methodist Church began in the United States in 1784, one of its first acts was the creation of Cokesbury College. Members of The Evangelical United Brethren tradition were equally zealous educators, as the presence of Otterbein and Albright Colleges testifies. People of the Methodist tradition were challenged to bring educational opportunity to the frontier; as a result, the people established approximately 1,200 schools across the North American continent. In 1913, the first Wesley Foundation was founded on the campus of the University of Illinois.

Today, the family of United Methodist-related institutions includes 10 major research universities, 13 seminaries, 80 liberal arts colleges, seven two-year colleges, one professional medical school, and 10 college preparatory schools. These are spread across the United States. The map on page 13 will help you locate them. Additionally, there are more than 520 campus ministries located on public and private college and university campuses across the country.

Our involvement in higher education reflects the social concerns of The United Methodist Church. Several institutions were founded especially for women. (In 1836, Wesleyan College in Macon, Georgia, was the first college in the world chartered to grant baccalaureate degrees to women.) Others were founded for African Americans. (By 1867, two years after the Civil War ended, 59 institutions had been founded to educate freed slaves.) These institutions were founded during a time when it was neither popular nor widely expected that women and African Americans should have educational opportunities. There are now 3 colleges for women and 11 historically Black colleges related to The United Methodist Church. United Methodist higher education provides greater access to more students through the largest network of Protestant institutions in the nation.

The church is involved in higher education—education for the common good, challenging faithful people to develop faithful minds for faithful life in the world.

Commitments and Common Themes of United Methodists in Higher Education

the United Methodist Church has a historic and impressive history in higher learning. Today, the family of United Methodist-related institutions includes 10 major research universities, 13 seminaries, 82 liberal arts colleges, seven two-year colleges, one professional medical school, and 10 college preparatory schools. These are spread across the United States. The map on page 13 will help you locate them.

Our involvement in higher education reflects the social concerns of The United Methodist Church. Several institutions were founded especially for women. (In 1836, Wesleyan College in Macon, Georgia, was the first college in the world chartered to grant baccalaureate degrees to women.) Others were founded for African Americans. (By 1867, two years after the Civil War ended, 59 institutions had been founded to educate freed slaves.) These institutions were founded during a time when it was neither popular nor widely expected that women and African Americans should have educational opportunities.

There are now 3 colleges for women and 11 historically black colleges related to The United Methodist Church. A total of 122 currently in the family gives United Methodism the highest Protestant presence in higher education in the nation. The strong variety of institutions contributes significantly to student access, equity, and democracy in higher education in the United States.

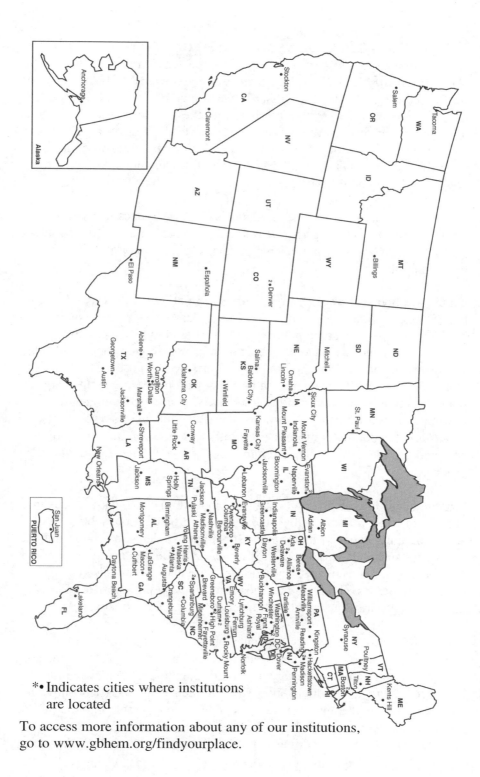

*• Indicates cities where institutions
  are located

To access more information about any of our institutions,
go to www.gbhem.org/findyourplace.

Campus and Collegiate Ministry

Campus ministry represents, in many ways, the "church beyond itself." (See *Campus Ministry: The Church Beyond Itself* by Donald G. Shockley, former staff at the General Board of Higher Education and Ministry; the resources list begins on page 23.) When the church reaches outside itself, it fulfills its mission to be involved fully in the life of the world. Ministry on campus is work that makes an impact both on the present-day lives of those on campus as well as on the future health of the church. Campus ministry is vital to both the church and the world.

United Methodist ministry with students is diverse. It takes many forms and offers many different programs. It is versatile, reaching a variety of student populations; and it is vital, reaching people who might not otherwise be touched by the church.

United Methodists sponsor campus ministry in at least four ways. First, we have Wesley Foundations and Fellowships—United Methodist campus ministry centers—on some publicly supported and independent college campuses. Second, we have ecumenical units—those we support together with other denominations—on public and private campuses. Third, college and university chaplains engage in ministry with the entire campus at United Methodist-related institutions. Finally, many local congregations now extend their ministries to embrace nearby colleges. As a result of these varied expressions of ministries with students, you may more often hear and use the term "collegiate ministries" to be inclusive of all these groups.

What happens in collegiate ministry may look similar to what happens in other ministries: worship, Bible study, service projects, counseling, classes, and community events. Much time is spent with students in groups and one-on-one for spiritual development. However, as student populations become older and their needs change, the ministry with and to them also changes. Groups for singles, childcare facilities, and fellowship groups for international students are some additional facets of collegiate ministries.

Collegiate ministry focuses on students, but it also has a broader campus focus. Faculty, staff, and administrators are the most stable parts of the college population. Often, working with and through them, collegiate ministry is able to reach many more people. Through their work and friendship with college personnel, campus ministers are able to draw people into unique programs: teachers of engineering helping to rehabilitate low-income housing, medical educators working with those in our country and in other countries who cannot afford health care, and law students and faculty lending their services to persons who cannot afford legal counsel.

From student movements to faculty study, from prayer breakfasts to social service, from personal counseling to global concerns, campus ministry embodies the church's mission in the world.

United Methodist Student Movement (UMSM)

Christian students have a long history of leadership in the United Methodist Church spanning many generations.

The first Methodist Student Movement (MSM) was established in St. Louis in 1937; its last conference was held in Lincoln, Nebraska, in 1965. In the intervening years, opportunities for service were a significant part of the MSM. The lives of thousands of students were profoundly changed by these experiences, and a host of people went on to become recognized leaders in the church and in society, while countless others whose names are not generally know invested themselves in lives of witness and service.

In 1987, a national student conference was held, again in St. Louis. Following the success of that conference, through 2011, national leadership training events known as Student Forums were held each year. In 1996, during Student Forum at Oklahoma City University, a new student movement was created. The United Methodist Student Movement, a network of college students that extends across the United States, bridges ethnic and cultural boundaries and reaches out across the globe.

UMSM is open to all college students who are connected to The United Methodist Church through church, campus ministry, or college university affiliation and who are interested in growing together in discipleship and leadership for the sake of the church and the world.

In many areas, students come together regularly through statewide, annual conference, jurisdictional conference, and regional gatherings of UMSM. Each annual conference has an adviser, usually a campus minister or college chaplain. The movement is supported by staff of the Campus Ministry Section of the General Board of Higher Education and Ministry.

Beginning in 2012, a new event, called NEXT, becomes the biennial leadership development and student conference of UMSM. All interested college students are encouraged to attend. Through creative speakers, dynamic worship, and affinity-group discussions, NEXT will challenge and inspire students to consider and plan the next faithful steps for their vocations, their communities, the church, and the world. The biennial meeting of NEXT is held in November on even-numbered years.

On the website for the United Methodist Student Movement (www.umsm.org), you will find more information, including information about upcoming conferences such as NEXT; a directory of UMSM advisers; a directory of United Methodist-related campus ministry programs; and the UMSM online community where students can share comments and discuss current issues.

Black College Fund

In 1865 when the Civil War ended, more than four million people who had been denied education were left to an unknown future. In a slavery system where it had been against the law to teach slaves to read and write, the quest for education, food, and shelter emerged as critical components for survival and progress.

In 1866, Bishop Davis W. Clark helped the Methodist Episcopal Church (a forerunner of The United Methodist Church) found the Freedmen's Aid Society dedicated to establishing schools and colleges for freed slaves in the South. By 1867, fifty-nine schools had been founded in ten states.

Fifty years after its founding, the Freedmen's Aid Society had started thirty-four colleges, academies, and theological schools. Often begun as small schoolrooms, these institutions grew to become well-established undergraduate colleges and universities located primarily in the South.

Eleven of these colleges continue as historically black institutions related to The United Methodist Church: Bennett College for Women (Greensboro, North Carolina), Bethune-Cookman University (Daytona Beach, Florida), Claflin University (Orangeburg, South Carolina), Clark Atlanta University (Atlanta, Georgia), Dillard University (New Orleans, Louisiana), Huston-Tillotson University (Austin, Texas), Meharry Medical College (Nashville, Tennessee), Paine College (Augusta, Georgia), Philander Smith College (Little Rock, Arkansas), Rust College (Holly Springs, Mississippi), and Wiley College (Marshall, Texas).

These colleges and universities have produced a legacy of leadership. In 1956, Dr. Willa B. Player became the first African American woman to serve as president of a four-year liberal arts college in the United States (Bennett College in North Carolina). Claflin University, the oldest historically black college or university in South Carolina, was the first school in the state to welcome all students regardless of race or gender. Azie Taylor Morton, a graduate of Huston-Tillotson University in Texas, served as treasurer of the United States in the Carter administration. She is the only African American to hold this office. Meharry Medical College, founded in 1876, was the first medical school for African Americans in the United States.

Through the Black College Fund apportionment, United Methodists continue their significant and long-standing tradition of providing educational opportunities to an important segment of the U.S. population. The United Methodist Church supports the largest number of black colleges and universities of any church body in the United States.

The colleges supported by the fund provide direct access, nurture, and professional and spiritual training and guidance to a student population that, in the main, would remain underserved without them. Of the approximately 16,000 students enrolled in these colleges, 90 percent qualify for financial aid. Tuition is kept relatively low so students with low incomes may attend. And, these colleges are and always have been open to all.

Because of The United Methodist Church's historic commitment through the Black College Fund, educational access and academic and professional accomplishments continue to become realities for thousands of students of promise.

Methodist Global Education Fund for Leadership Development

In countries around the world, Christian congregations are growing rapidly. In Africa, 46 percent of the population is Christian. In Latin America, the number is 34 percent. In Asia, 22 percent are Christian. Christian churches welcome more than 1.4 billion members worldwide.

Leadership development for these growing churches is the goal of the Methodist Global Education Fund for Leadership Development. By providing resources to meet the growing needs of these churches and people, we can also help guide the communities in which they are located. We have the opportunity to foster a sense of global connectedness that could allow millions of Methodists to share their knowledge, their energy, and their faith. The developing worldwide network of Methodist schools, colleges, universities, and theological schools training future leaders requires continuing nurture. Today, there are more than 700 Methodist educational institutions in nations around the world that work with Methodist congregations "to give the key of knowledge" to those who have very limited access to education.

The Methodist Global Education Fund for Leadership Development uses United Methodism's worldwide educational network to nurture the development of leaders who will foster local and worldwide communities that are peaceful, tolerant, and value-based. The fund is a unique opportunity to invest in the global community.

For more information, visit the website at www.gbhem.org/mgef, or contact the Division of Higher Education by e-mail scu@gbhem.org.

Africa University

Africa University, located in Old Mutare, opened in March 1992 as the first private, international university in Zimbabwe. This United Methodist-related university on the African continent was established by action of the 1988 General Conference. The university opened for classes with 40 students from a dozen African countries. Africa University currently has an enrollment of more than 1,300.

There are six faculties or colleges: theology, education, agriculture and natural resources, humanities and social sciences, health sciences, and management and administration. There are five postgraduate faculties: agriculture and natural resources; management and administration; theology; health sciences; and peace, leadership, and governance. The campus consists of five academic buildings, the university chapel, the library, a student union building, twelve residence halls, and ten faculty and staff houses.

Congregations and individuals across The United Methodist Church support Africa University. The university is a tangible witness to what The United Methodist Church can do to free people from poverty and transform people into leaders. One way your congregation can support Africa University is by paying 100 percent of the Africa University Fund apportionment. For more information about the Africa University Fund, visit www.umcgiving.org.

For more information about the university, contact the Africa University Development Office by e-mail at audevoffice@gbhem.org or by phone at 615-340-7438. Visit their website at www.support-africauniversity.org. The Africa University website is at www.africau.edu.

Office of Loans and Scholarships

The United Methodist Church Student Loan Program is the oldest and largest program of its type in America, serving students in higher education for more than a century. More than a half million students have realized their vocational dreams with financial assistance from The United Methodist Student Loan and Scholarship Programs. The program made its first loan in 1872 to a student preparing for a lay vocation,

The loan program operates as a revolving fund. As recipients repay their loans, the money is lent to other United Methodist students. The loan fund has a remarkable repayment rate of 99.5 percent.

The United Methodist Scholarship Program provides scholarships church-wide to supplement the financial needs of today's students. Funding for these scholarships is provided through offerings, wills, annuities, and other designated gifts.

To qualify for a scholarship, a student must be a full, active member of The United Methodist Church for at least a year before applying and be enrolled in a degree program at an accredited institution, maintaining a grade average of 2.5 or higher. To qualify for a loan, a student must be a full, active member of The United Methodist Church for at least one year prior to applying and must be enrolled in a degree program at an accredited institution, maintaining at least a C average.

In addition to these two types of assistance, the Office of Loans and Scholarships also administers several specialized scholarships. For information, go to www.gbhem.org. Some of these include:

- *The Gift of Hope Scholars Program* (for undergraduates who demonstrate strong leadership in the UMC)
- *Ethnic Minority Scholarship* (for undergraduates of Native American, Asian, African American, Hispanic, or Pacific Islander descent)
- *Brandenburg Scholarship* (for students thirty-five years of age or older)
- *The Edith Allen Scholarship* (for African American graduate or undergraduate students pursuing a degree in education, social work, medicine, or other health professions)
- *HANA Scholarship* (for students born of Hispanic, Asian, Native American, or Pacific Island parentage—either upper level undergraduate or graduate and doctoral students)
- *The Bishop James Baker Award* (for campus ministers)
- *The Rosalie Bentzinger Scholarship* (for deacons pursuing the PhD in Christian education)

• *The Special Seminary Scholarship* for students thirty years of age and under pursuing an MDiv degree at a United Methodist-related seminary or theological school.

Be sure to support these scholarships by observing United Methodist Student Day with an offering. Each year, this offering is a major source of funds for loans and scholarships. Ten percent of the Student Day offering is rebated each year to annual conferences participating in the Conference Merit Award Program.

In addition, 35 percent of the World Communion Sunday offering supports the Ethnic Minority Scholarship Fund. A portion of the offering receipts from Native American Ministries Sunday provides scholarships to Native-American United Methodist students pursuing a degree at a University Senate-approved school of theology.

Students can apply for a loan or scholarship by contacting the Office of Loans and Scholarships, PO Box 340007, Nashville, TN 37203; or by calling 615-340-7346 (loans) or 615-340-7344 (scholarships); or by visiting the website at www.gbhem.org. Persons who wish to endow a scholarship or loan in memory of a loved one may contact the Office of Loans and Scholarships at 615-340-7341.

United Methodist Higher Education Foundation

Founded in 1965, the United Methodist Higher Education Foundation (UMHEF) is dedicated to helping students achieve their dreams. UMHEF provides scholarship aid for United Methodist students attending the 122 United Methodist-related institutions. Its vision is to make it economically possible for any qualified United Methodist student to be educated at a United Methodist-related college or university.

Some UMHEF programs include:
• *United Methodist Dollars for Scholars* (The Foundation provides a $1,000 matching scholarship for churches that raise and provide $1,000 on behalf of student congregational members enrolled or planning to enroll in a United Methodist-related college, university, or seminary. In addition, there are *Triple Your Dollars* and *Quadruple Your Dollars* programs.)
• *United Methodist Leadership Scholars* (sponsored by United Methodist churches in the southeast and many United Methodist-related colleges and universities; designed to encourage active United Methodist students

to attend a United Methodist-related college by offering up to $3,000 in scholarship funds)

- The *September 11th Memorial Fund* (designed to provide assistance for surviving victims and dependents of victims of the terrorist attacks on September 11)

In addition, there is the "Named Scholarships" program that allows annual conferences, local churches, and other groups or individuals to establish a scholarship in honor or memory of a person. These gifts help young minds in the church acquire tools for a promising future, and make value-centered education accessible to all students. For information about making a gift to the Foundation, please visit the website at www.umhef.org. To speak with someone about making a gift, call 800-811-8110.

For more information, write the United Methodist Higher Education Foundation, PO Box 340005, Nashville, TN 37203-0005. Or call 800-811-8110. Visit the website at www.umhef.org.

Higher Education, Campus Ministry, and Your Local Church

there are countless ways your local church can have a vital and exciting ministry in higher education. In order to make this happen, be sure to keep the church council aware of the concerns of colleges, universities, and campus ministries. Interpret this ministry by personalizing it. As you describe programs, institutions, and causes, cite persons in your own congregation who have been affected by them.

Some members of your congregation may work for or be graduates of United Methodist schools and colleges, serve on their boards, or be members of the board of directors of a campus ministry. Identify members of your district or annual conference Board of Higher Education and Campus Ministry. Pay attention to the students in your congregation, some of whom worship with you and others who attend school away from home.
Listen to these people. Share their stories with the congregation and invite them to talk with others. They may have ideas for programs as well as helpful information to share with you and your local church.

What YOU Can Do—Here are some tangible ways to engage higher education and collegiate ministry:

1. As high school students begin to think about college, promote and visit United Methodist-related higher education institutions and campus ministries (www.gbhem.org/findyourplace), and provide information about United Methodist scholarships that are available from the local church, annual conference and general church (www.gbhem.org/loansandscholarships).
2. When students prepare to leave for college, share their names with the campus minister or chaplain at the school where they are enrolling (www.gbhem.org/findyourplace).
3. While students are away at college, keep in touch by adding them to the mailing or email list for the church newsletter, praying for them regularly, sending cards and care packages for semester final exams, and welcoming them home at winter and summer breaks.
4. Host special gatherings over Christmas break for returning students, invite students to participate in spring break mission experiences, and offer Bible studies and fellowship opportunities through the summer for those who are home.
5. Regularly educate your church about the United Methodist church's work in higher education through your church's bulletin board or website, worship time, and Sunday school classes. Provide information about the Black College Fund (www.gbhem.org/bcf), Africa University (www.africau.edu), and special offerings (www.umcgiving.org) such as United Methodist Student Day (November) and Native American Ministries Sunday (April).
6. If a United Methodist-related institution or campus ministry is nearby, invite students, faculty, staff, and collegiate ministers to participate in worship, lead or participate in special seminars, or utilize gifts of teaching, music, drama, or speaking in the church. Plan a recognition service and reception for all who are engaged in the ministry of higher education.
7. Support local collegiate ministries with prayers, financial support, notes of encouragement, and gifts of meals or service.
8. Offer extraordinary hospitality to students. Provide a warm welcome, free meals, and pastoral care to students who are visiting for the first time or who begin to attend regularly. Help students connect with mentors and families in the church.
9. Use social media and campus fliers to publicize worship times and events for students. Publicize campus events that are open to the community to church members.
10. Contact the chaplain, campus minister, and international student office to see if there are students who won't be going home for Christmas or Thanksgiving, and provide hospitality for them.

Resources

General Resources

Unless otherwise noted, the following resources can be ordered from the Division of Higher Education of the General Board of Higher Education and Ministry, PO Box 340007, Nashville, TN 37203-0007. Some of these are also available at www.gbhem.org.

- *The Guidebook of Unted Methodist-Related Schools, Colleges, Universities, and Theological Schools.* A guide to selecting a college, with information about United Methodist schools, colleges, and universities as well as loan and scholarship information. Available from Cokesbury at 800-672-1789, or go to www.cokesbury.com.
- *Annual Conference Higher Education Support Data.* An annual compilation of annual conference financial support of campus ministry, the Black College Fund, colleges and universities, and loans and scholarships. To find out about your annual conference's contributions, contact the Division of Higher Education.

Resource by Ministry Area

THE BLACK COLLEGE FUND

Unless otherwise indicated, resources are available through United Methodist Communications at 888-UMC-3242. Please provide the code and quantity needed when calling.

- *The Black College Fund brochure.* Includes information and location of all United Methodist-related black colleges and universities, along with ten reasons to attend a historically black college.
- *The Black College Fund bookmark.* Lists facts and information about the eleven UM-related historically black colleges and universities.
- *Black College Fund bulletin inserts* (#85800306). "Contribute to the Legacy" is a celebration of the history of the Black College Fund. Available from United Methodist Communications (888-346-3862) or online at www.umcgiving.org.
- *Instruments of Change DVD.* This thirteen-minute DVD highlights some of the world's best and brightest students, their groundbreaking research, and forward-thinking majors. The eleven UM-related historically black colleges and universities supported by the Black College Fund are put in historical context through interviews with families, professors, and students. Their inspirational testimonies provide a rich portrait of the vitality and importance of these institutions. Available from the Black

College Fund Office or from United Methodist Communications (888-346-3862) or online at www.umcom.org.
- *Operation Athletic Ambassador.* A program in which your church hosts a visiting sports team from one of the historically black colleges. Contact the Black College Fund Office at www.gbhem.org/bcf.

EXPLORATION
Here's a chance for students in your church to spend three days with other young people—high-school seniors through age twenty-four—who are exploring ordained ministry. EXPLORATION is an informative and discerning weekend of worship, Bible study, prayer, workshops, and small group discussions. The event is held on a regular basis, as a national event in some years and by jurisdiction in other years. If you know students who are interested in ministry, tell them about EXPLORATION and help send them to the event. For information, visit www.gbhem.org/exploration.

CAMPUS MINISTRY

Unless otherwise noted, the following resources can be ordered from the Campus Ministry Section, General Board of Higher Education and Ministry, PO Box 340007, Nashville, TN 37203-0007; or call 615-340-7404; or visit the website at www.gbhem.org.
- *17 Ways to Welcome College Students.* This flier provides tried-and-true suggestions for your congregation to become a more welcoming place for college and university students. Free. Available in English, Spanish, and Korean.
- *Cartas del Corazon: Reflexiones sobre los Salmos. Estas reflexiones y oraciones sobre varios Salmos fueron escritas por alumnos universitarios y clérigos asignados a la tarea de la labor pastoral con alumnos universitarios auspiciado por la Iglesia Metodista Unida.* Available in print from the Campus Ministry Section or online at www.gbhem.org/campus ministry.
- *Letters from the Heart: Reflections on the Psalms.* These reflections and prayers on various Psalms were written by college and university students, as well as a campus minister, who are involved in campus ministries sponsored by The United Methodist Church. Available in print from the Campus Ministry Section or online at www.gbhem.org/campusministry.
- *Campus Ministry: The Church Beyond Itself* by Donald G. Shockley. This book gives an overview of campus ministry, outlines a theology of campus ministry, and makes the case for campus ministry as mission. Westminster John Knox Press, 1989.

- *Campus Ministry Matters.* E-newsletter produced by the Campus Ministry Section. For campus ministers, college chaplains, annual conference leaders, and other interested persons. Subscribe by contacting the Campus Ministry Section at www.gbhem.org/campmin.
- *ExploreCalling.org.* A website for high school students, college students, seminarians, and other young adults interested in exploring God's call in their lives. Includes resources, tools for spiritual formation, and upcoming events. A resource CD-ROM is also available. Request it by e-mail at explore@gbhem.org or at www.ExploreCalling.org.
- *The Christian as Minister: An Exploration into the Meaning of God's Call,* edited by Robert F. Kohler and Sharon Rubey. An introduction into the meaning of God's call to ministry, the vision for that ministry, and the opportunities The United Methodist Church offers to live out that call. ISBN 978-0-938162-98-8. Available from Cokesbury at 800-672-1789 or online at www.cokesbury.com.
- *Answering God's Call for Your Life: A Look at Christian Calls and Church Vocations,* by Robert Roth. A guide to help young people listen, discern, and understand God's call in their life and its meaning for their life's work. ISBN 978-0-938162-94-0. Available from Cokesbury at 800-672-1789 or online at www.cokesbury.com.
- *Awakened to a Calling: Reflections on the Vocation of Ministry,* by Ann Svennungsen and Melissa Wiginton. Abingdon Press, 2005. ISBN 978-068705-390-2. Eight sermons on vocation offer an important resource for high school and college students making vocational decisions.

SCHOOLS, COLLEGES, AND UNIVERSITIES

Unless otherwise noted, the following resources can be ordered from the Division of Higher Education, General Board of Higher Education and Ministry, PO Box 340007, Nashville, TN 37203-0007; or call 615-340-7402; or visit the website at www.gbhem.org.

- *Schools, Colleges, and Universities of The United Methodist Church.* A complete listing of higher education institutions related to The United Methodist Church. Includes a map of their locations. Available from the Division of Higher Education; also available on the website: www.gbhem.org/education.
- *Directory of the International Association of Methodist-Related Schools, Colleges, and Universities.* Lists over 750 institutions, representing 67 nations, related to the World Methodist Council. Free online at www.gbhem.org/gbhem/iamscu.html.

EXPLORECALLING.ORG

Explorecalling.org is a bridge between those exploring ministry as vocation and those who work as leaders or mentors in discernment and leadership development. The website invites people to consider God's call in their lives, and provides answers to questions about candidacy and ministry in The United Methodist Church. ExploreCalling.org has the latest resources for those who work with youth and young adults. Visitors to the site may sign up to receive updated information and highlighted features.

AFRICA UNIVERSITY

- *Africa University Fund "Hope" bulletin inserts* (86000206). Postcard bulletin inserts share the stories of three Africa University students and how studying at Africa University has helped them to discover hope for the future. Available from United Methodist Communications (888-346-3862) or online at www.umcgiving.org.
- *Africa University Fund "Hope" brochures* (86000407). Features students from Africa University, the only United Methodist degree-granting university in Africa. Available from United Methodist Communications (888-346-3862) or online at www.umcgiving.org.
- *Africa University Today.* A periodic newsletter highlighting the connection between Africa University and United Methodist congregations. Available from the Africa University Development Office at 615-340-7438 or by e-mail at audevoffice@gbhem.org.
- *Africa University on the Web.* To find out more about Africa University, visit the www.support-africauniversity.org.

LOANS AND SCHOLARSHIPS

Unless otherwise noted, the following resources can be ordered from the Office of Loans and Scholarships, General Board of Higher Education and Ministry, PO Box 340007, Nashville, TN 37203-0007; or call 615-340-7346 (for loans) or 615-340-7344 (for scholarships); or visit the website at www.gbhem.org.

- *United Methodist Loans and Scholarships Handbook.* Lists all loans and scholarships available, including criteria, deadlines, and applications. Includes loans and scholarships for undergraduate and graduate students. Also lists links with other United Methodist agencies and organizations that offer scholarships.
- *Loan and Scholarship Special Offering Days Envelopes and Posters.* Envelopes and posters for each of the UM special days: Native American Awareness Sunday, World Communion Sunday, and UM

Student Day Sunday. These may be ordered from United Methodist Communications at 888-346-3862, or online at www.umcgiving.org.
- *Women of Color brochure.* Outlines scholarships available to women of color who are PhD or ThD students.

IMPORTANT WEBSITES

www.gbhem.org—website of the General Board of Higher Education and Ministry

www.gbhem.org/education—Division of Higher Education Web pages

The Division of Higher Education of the General Board of Higher Education and Ministry Web pages provide information about and links to the following:

United Methodist-Related Schools, Colleges, Universities, and UM Theological Schools (with links to institutions' Web pages)
www.gbhem.org/education

Higher Education and Public Policy
www.gbhem.org/education
www.naicu.edu

United Methodist-Related Campus Ministries and Chaplaincies
www.gbhem.org/campmin

United Methodist Loans and Scholarship Program
www.gbhem.org/loansandscholarships

Special Sundays With Offerings
www.umcgiving.org

The Black College Fund
www.gbhem.org/bcf

The United Methodist Student Movement (UMSM)
www.umsm.org

ExploreCalling
www.ExploreCalling.org

Africa University
www.africau.edu
www.support-africauniversity.org
www.umcgiving.org

The United Methodist Higher Education Foundation
www.umhef.org

Interpreter Magazine
www.interpretermagazine.org

NOTES

NOTES

NOTES

NOTES

GUIDELINES FOR LEADING YOUR CONGREGATION